Original title:
A House Made of Gingerbread

Copyright © 2024 Creative Arts Management OÜ
All rights reserved.

Author: Nash Everly
ISBN HARDBACK: 978-9916-90-866-2
ISBN PAPERBACK: 978-9916-90-867-9

The Honeycomb Haven

In a land where candy grows,
Honeycomb walls in vibrant rows.
Marshmallow pillows, sweet delight,
Giggles echo through the night.

Lollipop trees sway side to side,
With gumdrop squirrels that love to hide.
Sugar-coated roofs that shine,
In this place where dreams align.

A Sweet Escape

Take a leap where sweets abound,
Chocolate rivers flow around.
Fudge-filled boats, let's set a sail,
In a world where cookies prevail.

Gummy bears dance with cheer,
Laughter rings, no hint of fear.
Jump on cakes with frosting swirls,
In this world of candy pearls.

Glorious Confections

Whipped cream clouds and sprinkles rain,
Taffy twisted, oh what a gain!
Lemon drops that twist and twirl,
In this realm, I give a whirl.

Chocolate hills, what a view!
Sugary flowers in every hue.
We'll frolic 'neath the lollipop sky,
Where no one ever says goodbye.

The Delicate Dreamscape

Dancing on a frosting lane,
Cotton candy clouds, just insane!
With jellybean roads to skip along,
Here we all belong, oh so strong.

Cupcake castles, sweet and grand,
Pudding puddles, oh how they stand!
A realm where laughter's never far,
Join me under the candy star.

Sugar Walls and Cinnamon Dreams

Sugar walls stand proud and bright,
With candy beams that shimmer light.
A sprinkle here, a dash of fun,
Laughing hearts and giggles run.

Chocolate rivers flow with glee,
Lollipop trees, oh what a spree!
Marshmallow clouds float in the sky,
While gummy bears all dance and fly.

Sweet Delights of a Winter Hearth

In winter's chill, we gather near,
Sipping cocoa, spreading cheer.
With sugar stars upon the ground,
Every nibble makes a sound.

A cinnamon stick waves goodbye,
While taffy squirrels race on by.
Frosting drips, a sweet surprise,
Even the cookies wear disguise.

Whispers of Frosted Eaves

Whispers float from frosted eaves,
Of cookie crumbles and sweet leaves.
Minty winds play hide and seek,
With gumdrop raindrops, peek-a-boo peak.

Frosty paints on windows glow,
While the ginger friends put on a show.
Candy canes on rooftops sway,
Who knew sweets could dance this way?

Candy Corners and Icing Roofs

In corners filled with chewy treats,
Where jellybeans and laughter meet.
The icing roofs are tall and grand,
Each bite understood, a tasty plan.

Syrupy smiles grace the door,
Tickled by sugar, we all want more.
The giggles echo, the joy immense,
In this land of sweet pretense.

Sweet Tooth's Secrets Unveiled

In a world of sugar, how do you bake?
Sugar walls sticky, we're on a break.
Candy canes stand tall, in a gleeful row,
Gumdrops like pebbles, put on a show.

Frosting spills over, a sugary sea,
Laughter erupts, like a sugar spree.
Chocolate chips hiding, don't make a peep,
Who knew that cookies could giggle and leap?

A Retreat of Frost and Flavor

Meringue roofs with a snowy peak,
Caramel rivers, everyone sneaks.
Licorice fences, twisted with care,
Whipped cream trees, a sight so rare.

Sours yell with a tangy refrain,
Peppermint whispers drive you insane.
Maple syrup ponds, we dive right in,
A flavor-filled retreat, let the fun begin!

Whispering Walls of Marzipan

Walls whisper secrets, sweet as a dream,
With buttercream faces, they giggle and beam.
Marzipan creatures dart to and fro,
Dance under sprinkles, oh what a show!

The roof's a delight, both crunchy and sweet,
Each step is a choice of caramel treat.
Sugarcoated laughter fills up the air,
In this whimsical place, there's joy everywhere!

Architectural Wonders of Sweets

Behold the structure, a sweet spectacle,
Chocolate bricks make it so delectable.
Gingerbread windows all gleam and glow,
Honeycomb skylights shining below.

Toffee balconies let you watch the fun,
Lollipop gardens bask in the sun.
A castle of cupcakes, oh what a feast,
In this land of treats, the laughter won't cease!

Peppermint Parlor

In a room where sweets abound,
Every chair is candy crowned.
Lollipops stand tall and bright,
Jellybeans dance in pure delight.

A chocolate fountain spills its cheer,
Marshmallows giggle, oh so near.
Sugarplum fairies flit about,
Spreading joy with every shout.

An Arcadia of Cookies

Oven warm with cookie bliss,
Doughy dreams we cannot miss.
Frosted roofs in colors bold,
Sprinkles spin tales to be told.

Gingerfolk twirl in their space,
Whiskers twitch in sugar race.
Chocolate chips like stars do gleam,
In this land of cookie dream.

The Chocolate Chalet

Nestled in a cocoa wood,
A cabin made of all things good.
Nutty beams and caramel walls,
Every corner sweetly calls.

Sipping cocoa by the fire,
Toasting marshmallows we aspire.
Chocolate bunnies hop with glee,
Inviting all to join their spree.

Sugared Shadows

In shadows sweet where secrets swish,
Gumdrop gnomes fulfill each wish.
Licorice vines twist and twirl,
Syrupy laughter starts to whirl.

Ginger kittens scamper fast,
With chocolate tails that leave a trail.
In this sugary land of chance,
Sweet dreams bloom with every glance.

Elysium in Edible Architecture

In a kingdom of candy, dreams take flight,
Where gumdrops glisten in the sun's bright light.
The roof is a cookie, the walls made of cake,
A nibble from here? Oh, for goodness' sake!

Licorice beams hold the structure so proud,
While marshmallow puffs form a fluffy white cloud.
My neighbors, the jellybeans, dance in delight,
As we feast on this sweetness, our hearts feel so light.

Spice-Laden Shadows of Home

Within walls of spice, the aroma's so grand,
With cinnamon whispers, a taste so well planned.
Each corner is painted with sugar so bright,
Where cookies are kept, out of mind—out of sight.

The tales of our meals could fill up a book,
With frosting and fondant, all ready to cook.
A sprinkle of laughter, the best ingredient,
In this cozy abode, we find fun and merriment.

Whimsical Abandon in Sugar's Embrace

In the land where the sweets make a charming parade,
There's licorice laughter and lemonade braid.
Chocolate fondant flows like a bubbling brook,
And cookies are stacked in a delightful nook.

The frosting smirks down from the eaves up above,
With candy cane pillars? We just feel the love.
A slide made of taffy, a merry-go-round,
In our joy-soaked oasis, pure happiness found.

The Sugarplum Sanctuary

In a realm where the sweets all gather and chat,
Our roof is a fudge, and our dog is a cat.
With cupcakes for cushions, we lay down to rest,
In a kingdom of treats, how could it be less?

The gumball machine serves as a makeshift chair,
While licorice strings weave laughter in the air.
Each visit with friends feels like a grand feast,
In our sugarplum haven, the fun never ceased.

The Cozy Confectionery Retreat

In a land where sweet dreams lay flat,
Cookies stack high, imagine that!
Chocolate rivers flow with glee,
Candy canes dance by the tree.

Marshmallow pillows, soft and bright,
Whipped cream clouds in the moonlight.
Lollipops swing on a breeze,
Sugary laughter among the trees.

Crystallized Echoes of Festivity

Gumdrop gates invite you near,
With sprinkles of joy and holiday cheer.
Frosted windows, a candy parade,
In this sweet world, we've got it made!

Jelly bean walls in radiant hues,
A feast of flavors, you choose your muse.
Giggling gingersnap kids run around,
In this sugary kingdom, joy knows no bound.

The Ginger Pie Haven

A crust of laughter fills the air,
With pies that make you stop and stare.
Marzipan moons shine down so bright,
As sugar sprites dance with delight.

Cinnamon whispers tickle your nose,
While caramel rivers softly flow.
Tarts and treats from every nook,
Grab a slice and have a look!

Caramelized Memories of Yesteryears

In the pantry of time, sweet tales reside,
Sticky fingers and laughter coincide.
Nostalgia wraps round like soft taffy,
Bringing back moments that make us happy.

Toffee secrets from days gone by,
Choco-chip stories that make us sigh.
In every crumb, there's a giggle or two,
With each sweet bite, we start anew.

Frosted Elysium

In a land where sweetness reigns,
Marshmallow clouds and caramel lanes.
Gummy bears stand guard with glee,
Bouncing on jellybean tramps, oh me!

Fudge rivers flow with creamy delight,
Chocolate trees reach a sugary height.
Lollipops dance in a minty breeze,
Inviting all to munch as they please.

Candied paths twist with laughter and cheer,
Every corner echoes, 'Eat over here!'
Gingersnap squirrels dance without a care,
Nibble a branch, just breathe in the air!

Here, calories never count, it's true,
Sweets are the law, decree number two.
In this merry realm where giggles abound,
Every bite is a slice of joy found.

The Cakewalk Castle

With frosting turrets standing tall,
This confectionery wonder calls.
Waffle cones serve as regal towers,
And cheesecake gardens bloom for hours.

Marzipan knights in sugar coats,
Greet every guest with sugary floats.
Jelly moat protects from outside woes,
While gummy worms tie up the bows.

Caramel drawbridge dips down low,
Cherries on high in rows to show.
Every hallway whispers a sweet tune,
Under the glaze of a fondant moon.

In this bizarre and frosted space,
Every laugh draws a new silly face.
Where everything's flavored, from walls to floor,
Join the feast, there's always room for more!

Sugar-Spun Reverie

In a dream spun from sticky delight,
Candy clouds float in a sugary light.
Biscuit beams and toffee streams,
Swirling together like wild-flavored dreams.

Cinnamon chairs fluff up with cream,
Popcorn pillows burst at the seam.
Lemon lollies line the sweet lane,
Tickling your senses, driving you insane.

Frosting fountains bubble with cheer,
Sprinkles rain down, always near.
In this whimsical space of fun,
Every appetite is never outdone.

Sugar rush, laughter flares bright,
Dancing with cupcakes until the night.
Off to the land where dessert makes sense,
Come share a moment in this sweet suspense.

The Scrumptious Sanctuary

Under a sky of candy canes,
Chocolate streams run through jelly plains.
In this fortress of dessert true,
Every nibble is plated for you.

Licorice logs lie by the door,
Gingerbread curtains flutter and soar.
Meringue maids serve pies on a tray,
As you giggle and munch all day.

Cookie crumbles fill the streets,
With candy corn buzzing, life is sweet.
Every step leads to a shocking treat,
Marshmallow peeps dance to the beat.

So, come along, don't be shy,
Join the fun beneath sugar-tipped sky.
In this whimsical refuge of flair,
Give in to laughter, without a care!

Luscious Landscapes

In a land where sweetness flows,
And candy blossoms brightly grow,
The gumdrop path begins to sway,
With licorice trees on display.

Choco rivers twist and churn,
As candy critters take their turn,
They giggle as they skedaddle by,
While frosting clouds float in the sky.

A frosty wind brings whispers sweet,
Of sugary dreams where all can greet,
The jellybean doors creak with glee,
In this land of pure jubilee.

With lollipops like tall lampposts bright,
This place is surely pure delight,
Here, every nibble sparks a cheer,
Join the fun, the feast is near!

The Sifted Sugar Stratum

In a pantry, flour takes a leap,
As sugar dust begins to creep,
The whiskers dance, the spatula twirls,
In a world where chaos unfurls.

A sprinkle fight breaks out with flair,
Marshmallow clouds float in the air,
With frosting as the soldier's cape,
They battle till the cookies shape.

The cinnamon stars watch from above,
While confectionery creatures play and shove,
With giggles that are sweet and loud,
They cheer for cake in a sugary crowd.

At last, they gather in a pile,
With buttercream smiles, they reconcile,
In this realm where laughter rings,
Sugar-coated joy is all that springs.

The Sprinkle Sanctuary

Here lies a joy of vibrant hues,
With rainbow sprinkles and sweetened views,
They twinkle on every cupcake spine,
While gummy bears declare, "This is divine!"

Chocolate fountains bubble with glee,
Marshmallow bunnies dance with tea,
In a world where laughter rounds the bend,
The cookie companions make amends.

With licorice whips that twist and shout,
And candy canes that prance about,
A jellybean chorus starts to sing,
While frosted dreams take to wing.

When day is done and dusk arrives,
The peanut brittle hive comes alive,
In this sanctuary of sugary fun,
Everyone's a winner, nobody's done!

The Oven's Embrace

In the warmth of a cozy nook,
Baking dreams in every book,
The oven hums a favorite tune,
As batter rises like a balloon.

A whisk gets dizzy, and spoons align,
While chocolate chips dance in a line,
Glazed donuts twirl, quite a sight,
As the kitchen turns to pure delight.

The timer dings, a happy shout,
As frosted treats come racing out,
Sprinkles flying here and there,
A sugar rush beyond compare.

Now scrap the crumbs, let laughter soar,
In the oven's love, there's always more,
With cupcakes bright and cookies fat,
We celebrate with a pitter-pat!

Threads of Sweetness

In a land where the gumdrops grow,
Chocolate rivers flow, oh what a show!
With frosting beams and a licorice floor,
We laugh and we snack, always wanting more.

The roof is a swirl of bright candy canes,
Beneath every eave, a sprinkle of grains.
We dance through the halls with sugar in tow,
In this land of delight, there's always a glow.

With jellybean doors that jiggle and jive,
We wonder how long the sugary thrive.
The windows are lollipops, glossy and bright,
Inside, joyful giggles echo through the night.

As the sun sets low over icing so sweet,
We feast on our dreams with a frosting treat.
In this whimsical world spun of candy art,
The laughter we share is a genuine part.

The Crushed Candy Keepsake

I found a treasure, a sugary slice,
A cookie memento, oh isn't it nice?
It crumbled to bits at the very first bite,
Yet brought all the sweetness, a hilarious sight.

A peppermint door, it squeaks as it breaks,
With every small step, it shimmers and shakes.
A blast of confetti, oh what a thrill,
As sprinkles take flight, they blow from the hill.

A pop of a gumdrop, a pitter-pat sound,
This crispy facade just can't hold its ground.
As laughter erupts with the sugary crash,
We treasure these moments, a colorful splash.

In the chaos, we giggle, we'll savor each bite,
Of our quirky keepsake, a true delight.
Though it fades in a blink, in memory stays,
The joy we've created in candied arrays.

Ginger Snap Groves

In the grove of the snaps, where the ginger folks play,
They jiggle and wiggle in a delightful display.
With icing as bubbles, they bounce to the beat,
It's a dance of the sweets, oh what a treat!

The trees sway with cookies, the leaves made of fondant,
Giggling gingerbread friends who are utterly gallant.
They challenge the breeze with a crusty high kick,
It's silly, it's sweet, and it's all done real quick.

Oh, care for the gingers and candy implore,
They'll share their delights, but just don't take more!
With smiles dipped in frosting, they jump and they cheer,
In the grove of the snaps, laughter's always near.

So come join the fun, bring your silly hat too,
Let's frolic like cookies and dance on the dew.
For in this sweet land, every moment will gleam,
As we savor the laughter, wrapped tight in a dream.

Flavors of Fantasy

In a land where sweets do grow,
Candy flowers put on a show.
Marshmallow clouds float high and wide,
Lollipop trees on every side.

Chocolate rivers happily flow,
Gummy bears put on a row.
Ice cream cones make the sunbeam,
Jellybeans dance in a swirl and dream.

Sugar roads lead to the feast,
Where jelly rolls are quite the least.
Fudge fountains start to drip,
And cupcake bridges take a trip.

Sprinkles rain from skies so bright,
Every taste is pure delight.
A world where fun is always near,
In this land, we have no fear!

Sugarplum Sanctuary

In a nook where sweets reside,
Sugarplums with arms spread wide.
Taffy critters laugh and play,
In this realm, it's always a buffet.

Honeyed whispers greet you there,
Marzipan critters steal a stare.
Cookies giggle as they bake,
Every breath is a sugary shake.

Cupcake fairies flit about,
Sprinkling joy without a doubt.
Gumdrop paths to frolic on,
Join the dance from dusk till dawn.

Frosting rivers don't run dry,
Where peppermint clouds drift on high.
A jolly sight where flavors blend,
In this land, let's not pretend!

The Tasty Trove

In a corner of the sweetly bright,
Cookies twinkle in the light.
Biscuit bricks stack to the sky,
Gingerbread folks with a wink and sigh.

Candy canes stand straight and tall,
While caramel rivers gently call.
Every creak and every crack,
Tells a tale of snack-filled tracks.

Fruity treasures hide and seek,
Brownie towers peek a peek.
Delicious sighs fill the air,
In this trove, there's love to share.

Chocolate chips race all around,
Where the happiest tunes are found.
Savor each laugh and each bite,
In the trove of pure delight!

The Icing on the Roof

On the top where the sweets conspire,
Icing dreams reach up higher.
Every layer's a frosted cheer,
Meringue monkeys swing from here.

Ginger snaps run all aglow,
While cotton candy drifts below.
Strawberry sunbeams fill the space,
Laughing loudly in their place.

Pastry peaks point to the sky,
As taffy twirls and fluffs up high.
Sundae clouds float gently by,
In this land, we laugh and sigh.

Cookies watch the silly play,
With sprinkles shining bright and gay.
In this whimsy, we let loose,
Let's celebrate this sweet excuse!

Molasses Whispers

In the land where sweetness drips,
With gumdrop dreams and icing sips,
The walls are thick with sugary cheer,
Yet ants dance in, oh dear, oh dear!

Chocolate beams and marzipan frames,
Bubblegum laughter, wild candy games,
Strawberry doors that swing with delight,
At night, the lollipops glow in the light.

Treacle Tranquility

Honey drips from every seam,
The windows sparkle like a dream,
Cinnamon rooves that gently sway,
A cozy nook for a cookie play.

Gumdrops tumble down the lane,
Sugar rushes can't be contained,
Minty breezes swirl and twirl,
In this sweet shop, joy unfurls!

The Scrambled Sweets Abode

Peppermint sticks hold up the sky,
With jellybean clouds drifting by,
Every corner's a flavor surprise,
Where the cupcakes chuckle and pies capsize.

Pudding puddles serve as pools,
Chocolate chip chairs and waffle stools,
Beneath the rainbow gumdrop tree,
Life's a treat, oh what glee!

Frosty Facades

Icicles hang like candy cane lights,
The roof's a cake of frosted delights,
Licorice fences, a cherry path,
Where laughter erupts in sweet aftermath.

Cotton candy fluff in the breeze,
Bouncing marshmallows dance with ease,
In this realm of frosty fun,
Every nibble's a sugary run!

Edible Wonders

In a land where sweets don't fade,
Walls of candy, brightly made.
Lollipops dance, twirl in the sun,
Gumdrop gardens, oh what fun!

Licorice lanes weave here and there,
Sugar rooftops, sweet scents in air.
Chocolate rivers flow, oh so wide,
Frosting clouds, a sugary ride!

Mice made of marzipan run wild,
Jellybean treasures, oh so reviled.
Gingersnap critters scamper with glee,
In this land where calories flee!

So come take a stroll, do not delay,
In this candy kingdom, we all want to play.
With every bite, laughter spills free,
In a world where we all just want to be!

Spiced Secrets

In the pantry, secrets hide,
Ginger and nutmeg, side by side.
Whispers of cinnamon swirl in the air,
Tickling noses, everywhere!

Frosted windows, a sweet surprise,
Marshmallow fluff, a sugary prize.
The walls giggle, just wait and see,
What's hiding behind the chocolate tree!

Sweet licorice swings, oh so grand,
Candy canes grow like a band.
Sprinkles sprinkle laughter all around,
In every corner, joy can be found!

You might stumble, take a bite,
Discover secrets that feel so right.
In this flavorful land, come join the cheer,
For laughter is sweeter with candy near!

Crumbs of Joy

Each crumb dances, leaps, then lands,
Sprinkling giggles across the sands.
Chocolate chips with a wink and a tease,
Bring joy to hearts, as they please!

Frosting rivers flow with delight,
Cookie clouds drift off into night.
Gummy bears pluck strings of glee,
As they strum on the caramel tree!

In this place where flavors sing,
Sugar fairies take to the wing.
Every bite is a ticket to fun,
A laughter ride that's never done!

So grab a spoon, don't be afraid,
In this wonderland, thoughts cascade.
With every nibble, joy will sprout,
In sweetness abundant, there's no doubt!

Confectioner's Delight

Beneath the frosting, a tale unfolds,
Of sweet escapades that never get old.
Caramel whispers, secrets to share,
In each little bite, joy's everywhere!

Taffy tug-of-war, oh what a sight,
Tootsie rolls flying, oh such a fright!
The licorice vines stretch high in the sky,
With jellybeans laughing as they fly by.

Gingerbread houses, sugary dreams,
Filled with the laughter of frosting beams.
The air is thick with sweet, fluffy cheer,
In this land of sweets, I have no fear!

So let's gather round, bring your spoon,
Join the fun, let's dance to the tune.
In a world so sweet, we're all in flight,
With each bite taken, pure delight!

A Whisk of Fantasy

In a land where sweets reside,
Chocolate rivers, gumdrop tide,
Lollipop trees that sway and spin,
Dance beneath the candy skin.

Ginger critters hop with glee,
Frosting smiles on all they see,
Licorice roads lead to delight,
Sugar dreams that last all night.

Marshmallow clouds float so high,
Sprinkle stars adorn the sky,
A realm of treats both bold and bright,
Where laughter sparkles with the light.

Join the feast, don't hesitate,
Sour sweets that twist your fate,
In this world, we're free to play,
Savor joy in every way.

Flavorful Illuminations

Candied windows glow so sweet,
Living where the gumdrops meet,
Lemonade flows with zing and cheer,
Sugar fairies always near.

With licorice pipes puffing high,
Fudge balloons float in the sky,
Baking magic fills the air,
While cookie ghosts dance without a care.

Peppermint winds whittle around,
Jellybean hearts begin to astound,
Each flavor tells a silly tale,
Follow the marshmallow trail.

Salted caramel rain will pour,
Life is sweet and never a bore,
In this world, giggles reign supreme,
Indulge in every tasty dream.

The Treat Tapestry

A tapestry of sweet delight,
Fruity wonders, colors bright,
Gummy bears and chocolate lace,
Grinning candies all in place.

In the oven, giggles rise,
Pies that wobble, filled with skies,
Every crumb tells tales that cheer,
Laughter echoes far and near.

Candy canes like striped tall trees,
Whipping cream, a gentle breeze,
Joyful moments, syrupy fun,
A sprinkle dash, the good times run.

Nibble treats, don't waste a space,
In this laugh-filled, sugar race,
Dip in laughter, take a bite,
It's a feast for pure delight.

Whipped Whimsy

Whipped up chaos on a plate,
Creamy dreams that can't be late,
Silly owls in cookie hats,
Pancake stacks and dancing rats.

Pudding pools and jelly joys,
Search for giggles, girls and boys,
Fizzy drink showers, what a blast,
Breakfast time, but nobody's fast.

Cream cheese clouds, a fluffy cheer,
Scones that vanish, disappear,
Chocolate streams bubbled with fun,
Sour candy drivers on the run.

Laughing pies in a fruity race,
Every bite a sweet embrace,
In this world where giggles churn,
Silly whims and lessons learned.

The Lollipop Lodge

In a land where candies meet,
A lodge stands on a sugary street.
With walls of lollipops, bright and bold,
A sight so sweet, it never gets old.

Marshmallow pillows, fluffy and round,
Where gummy bears hop, oh what a sound!
Chocolate rivers flow with delight,
In this place, every day feels bright.

Peppermint windows, oh what a view,
Cupcake roofs with frosting so new.
A place where laughter fills the air,
With candy canes dancing everywhere!

So come, my friend, take a bite,
Join the fun till day turns to night.
In this whimsical lodge, don't be shy,
Savor the sweets and let out a sigh!

A Retreat of Treats

There's a retreat where goodies play,
A sweet escape from the grim day.
With licorice vines that twist and twine,
And rivers of soda, oh how they shine!

Gingerbread folks dance on the floor,
They shuffle and slide, asking for more.
Candy corns sing, oh what a tune,
Under a marshmallow sun and a chocolate moon.

Popcorn clouds float in the sky,
While jellybeans bounce, oh my, oh my!
In this retreat, joy knows no bounds,
With laughter and sweetness in happy sounds.

So pack your bags, it's quite a treat,
Join the fun on this sugary street.
A place where smiles blossom and bloom,
In this retreat, you'll banish all gloom!

An Architecture of Flavor

In a realm where sweetness takes flight,
An architecture of flavor, oh what a sight!
With candy bricks and frosting fair,
Every nook sings with sugary air.

The licorice ladder leads up high,
To gummy bear clouds drifting by.
A landscape dressed in sugary hues,
Where laughter erupts like fizzy sodas do.

Chocolate beams hold up the roof,
As caramel drizzles tell the truth.
This structure's designed by a child at play,
In a world where sweets rule the day.

So let your imagination roam free,
In this realm of endless glee.
An architecture of laughter and cheer,
Where every bite brings joy near!

The Cookie Cottage

In a quaint little nook, there hides,
A charming cottage with cookie sides.
With chocolate chip tiles that glimmer and shine,
This cozy spot is simply divine!

Oreo shutters, designed to impress,
Under a roof of powdered sugar excess.
In the yard, a cupcake garden blooms,
With sprinkles that dance, banishing glooms.

The gingerbread door swings open wide,
Inviting all for a fun joyride.
Here, laughter echoes between the walls,
As sweet treats tumble, nobody stalls!

So take a step inside this realm,
Where happiness is at the helm.
In the cookie cottage, fun never stops,
Join the feast—come on, let's swap!

Candied Capriccio

In a world where sweets reside,
Chocolate rivers, candy tide.
Lollipop trees sway in the breeze,
Gumdrop gardens, oh what a tease!

Sugar clouds float, fluffy and bright,
Licorice paths lead to pure delight.
Candy corn characters dance with glee,
Join the party, it's sweet jubilee!

Marshmallow moons in a frosting sky,
Every bite makes you want to fly.
Gingerbread bricks with icing so fine,
Every corner's a taste of divine!

Join the fun, don't just observe,
In this sugary world, let's swerve.
With every laugh and giggly cheer,
We'll savor this treat, year after year!

The Caramel Cove

In the cove where sweet waves crash,
Toffee surfboards, full of splash.
Caramel sun shines down so bright,
It drips and dribbles, quite the sight!

Fudge-tasting sand on a licorice shore,
Every grain begs to be explored.
Candy canes line the path so sweet,
With each step, it's a sugary treat!

Gummy fish swim in syrupy pools,
Join the fun, forget the rules!
Lollipop boats sail the gooey sea,
In this land, we'll always be free!

When the sun sets in jellybean hues,
We'll dance with delight in our candy shoes.
Every giggle in the soft, sticky air,
Makes the Cove a land beyond compare!

Aroma of Delight

Whiff of frosting fills the air,
Baking dreams beyond compare.
Ginger whirls as spices play,
In this kitchen, joy's on display!

Cupcake clouds and pie plate moons,
Silly songs and baking tunes.
Sprinkle fairies flutter by,
Their giggles make the pastries fly!

Molasses rivers, rich and sweet,
With cookie boats that can't be beat.
Choco-chips whisper "let's have fun,"
In this aroma, we all are one!

Watch the laughter rise like bread,
With every pinch, joy's been spread.
In this kitchen of pure delight,
We'll bake our dreams, from day to night!

Tasting the Architecture

Come explore the great design,
With icing roofs on which we dine.
Ginger beams that hold it true,
With marshmallow pillows, just for you!

Every corner, a gummy surprise,
In this structure, laughter flies.
Lemon doors with candy locks,
Beneath the eaves, a chocolate box!

Twisted taffy columns stand tall,
Come and munch, don't let it fall.
Tasting walls, it's quite the feat,
With each bite, it's oh-so sweet!

At dinner here, the fun will beam,
Table set like a sugary dream.
In this whimsical tasty spree,
We bite the walls to feel so free!

An Oasis of Icing

In a land where sweets abound,
Candy canes grow from the ground.
Chocolates rain down from the sky,
Gummy bears bounce as they fly.

Sprinkles shimmer like stars at night,
Frosting fountains flow with delight.
Lollipops dance to a sugary tune,
Chocolate bunnies giggle in June.

Marshmallow clouds fluff up the air,
Jellybean flowers bloom everywhere.
Licorice roots twist and twine,
A dessert paradise, simply divine!

Here, every nibble brings silly grins,
Where frostings swirl then twirl and spin.
Life's a treat, come take a bite,
In this place, everything feels right.

Whimsy in Whipped Cream

There's a castle made of fluff,
With a moat of cream, oh so tough!
Velvet couches of gooey fudge,
Where candy critters never judge.

Peanut butter doors swing wide,
With jelly-filled windows, a silly ride.
Froggie friends hop with delight,
In this sweet realm, all feels right.

Giggles echo through syrupy halls,
As cookie kids play silly ball.
Life here never has a frown,
With cherry pies wearing crowns!

Cupcake towers touch the sky,
While gummy worms slide and fly.
With a swirl of whipped cream glee,
This whimsical world's the place to be!

The Marzipan Manor

Step into a charming abode,
Where almond dreams burst and explode.
Walls made of fondant, oh so sweet,
Sipping lemonade, what a treat!

Cinnamon windows that open wide,
With musky scents wafting inside.
As peppermint fairies flit about,
Laughing loudly, there's never doubt.

Overhead, gumdrop chandeliers,
Shining bright, igniting cheers.
Sugarplum pathways lead the way,
In this silly space where we play!

Here, every room sings a song,
Where chocolate walls can't go wrong.
A delightful feast, we gather round,
In this manor, joy is found!

A Retreat in Spice

In a nook where flavors collide,
Spiced cookies stand with great pride.
Clove-scented breezes softly sway,
While gumdrops giggle, come what may.

Cinnamon swirls fill each hall,
And ginger folks on gingerbread crawl.
Here in this cozy, fragrant bliss,
Every moment is a playful kiss.

Fruity truffles hang from the trees,
Where licorice lizards dance with ease.
Charming spice floats in the air,
As sugary laughter spits everywhere!

Let's raise our glasses, toast with cheer,
In this retreat, there's nothing to fear.
With every bite, let's spread the fun,
In our peppered paradise, we're never done!

Golden Glaze

In a world where sweets collide,
With icing rivers flowing wide,
Sugar dust on every ledge,
I smiled at my candy hedge.

Gummy bears on the front lawn,
They wiggle and dance at the dawn,
A lollipop sun in the sky,
Jellybeans buzzing nearby.

Chocolate squirrels scamper fast,
Hiding sweets in a marshmallow cast,
Licorice vines twist and twine,
In this land where treats align.

Candied dreams fill the air,
With fluffy clouds, we all share,
No worries here, just sticky glue,
Let's eat our way to the moon, woohoo!

The Pastry Pavilion

Welcome to the pastry show,
Where cupcakes twirl and rivers flow,
Frosting mountains stacked up high,
Watch the syrup streams go by.

Here, the tarts laugh with delight,
And pie crusts come alive at night,
They dance around in sugar-fueled glee,
Celebrate with whipped cream tea!

A croissant slides down the hill,
The muffin's giggles give a thrill,
With sprinkles raining from the sky,
Each pastry yields a happy sigh.

Ginger cookies in a race,
Zooming round at a scary pace,
In this pavilion of sweet refrain,
Life's a treat and not mundane!

Whirling Confections

Round and round, the gumdrops spin,
As candy canes begin to grin,
Marshmallow bunnies hop in sync,
With chocolate rivers, what do you think?

Pirouetting sugar plums swarm,
In the sweet chaos, they keep warm,
A carousel of gummy delight,
Bouncing happily every night.

The licorice ropes whip and sway,
Making us laugh, come what may,
Strawberry clouds throw cotton candy,
In a whirlwind, oh so dandy!

With frosting spritzers and candy sails,
We burst out giggling at sugary fails,
This land of whimsy never ends,
Join the dance, grab your friends!

The Marzipan Maze

In the maze made of sweet delight,
Wander candy paths, pure delight,
Marzipan walls, so smooth and sweet,
Where every corner has a treat.

Lollipop lanterns brightly shine,
Leading us down this path divine,
With chocolate puddles on the floor,
I never knew I'd want to explore!

Jellybean critters lead the way,
Through candy fields where we can play,
Join the fun, let giggles flow,
In the maze of sweets, let's go!

But beware of the taffy traps,
Where gumballs launch and leave you gaps,
Yet together we'll find a way,
Through the maze we joyfully sway!

The Dulcet Dwelling

In a place where sweet treats clatter,
Where frosting drips and laughter splatters,
A roof of sprinkles, bright and bold,
Tells tales of sugar, stories told.

Pillars of candy, sturdy and round,
The funniest quirks can always be found.
Lollipop lamps that light up the night,
Spark joy in every silly bite.

Gingerbread walls with gumdrop glue,
Each corner filled with a whimsical view.
Rooms frosted pink with a sugary scent,
It's never too much, the kids are content.

A garden of jellybeans grown with care,
Giggling squirrels nibble here and there.
With chocolate paths and marshmallow grass,
Laughter echoes, oh what a class!

Gummy Bears and Glazed Eaves

Under a ceiling of soft candy sheen,
Where gummy bears dance, oh what a scene!
The windows are glazed, with sweet sticky pride,
Peeking inside, giggles can't hide.

Marshmallow fluff puffs in the air,
A sprinkle shower makes life a dare.
The eaves are drizzled with syrupy cheer,
Each nibble takes you far, oh dear!

A trampoline made from licorice floors,
Jump into laughter and open the doors.
Snack time is silly, with pie on the face,
In this land of fun, we're winning the race!

In a yard where cupcakes grow to be tall,
And caramel rivers just beckon us all.
Life is a party, with sweets at our feet,
In our comical kingdom, it's all just so sweet!

Windows of Wafer

Through windows of wafer, the world's a delight,
With cookies for curtains, all snug and tight.
Chocolate chip pillows and jellybean rugs,
Every room filled with laughter and hugs.

The roof is a biscuit, so crispy and light,
Raindrops roll off, what a glorious sight!
Sprinkles are falling like confetti on cheer,
While silly cats prance about with no fear.

Soda pop fountains and licorice swings,
Come join in the fun as the laughter rings.
With gumdrops for chairs and candy cane trees,
It's a wacky place, come do as you please!

Sunshine of syrup to sweeten the day,
While the children giggle, they'll laugh and play.
In a world made of sweets, every day is a treat,
With cookies for kisses, oh, what a sweet feat!

The Brown Sugar Bungalow

In the bungalow made of brown sugar cheer,
Where laughter is baked and fun is the gear.
Seats made of cake, with icing divine,
Everyone's smiling, oh, isn't it fine!

With walls that are warm and full of surprise,
Giant candy canes stretch to the skies.
Toffee treasures hiding in every nook,
Come here, open up your sweetest cookbook!

Marzipan flowers in the front yard sway,
While popcorn balloons over giggles play.
Biscuit walks lead to a fizzy delight,
In this playful paradise, dreams take flight.

Even the pets have a sugary twist,
Chocolate-chip kittens, oh, how can you resist?
So pack up your troubles and brace for the fun,
In the brown sugar haven, laughter's begun!

Chewy Foundations of Joy

In a land where cookies grow,
Gods of sugar, knead the dough.
Marshmallow roofs and jellybean walls,
Laughter echoes through candy halls.

Lollipops lean like tired trees,
Gumdrop pathways covered in bees.
Frosting rivers flow with glee,
Join the dance of sweet jubilee.

Chocolate rain falls from above,
As gummy bears sing songs of love.
Bouncing bows and licorice twirls,
Come frolic with us, all boys and girls.

Sour patch clouds softly drift,
In this world, there's a sugar rift.
When life is tough, just take a bite,
And everything will feel just right.

Tales from the Candyland Hideaway

Gather 'round for tales untold,
In a realm of sweets, where dreams unfold.
Hiding spots made of peppermint,
Laughter and treats are always meant.

Rabbits bounce on jelly-filled hills,
Candy canes provide the thrills.
A donut tree sways in the breeze,
Where everyone shares a sugary tease.

Fudge fudge, the night's sweet light,
Where every creature dances in delight.
A chocolate stream flows bright and bold,
As cookie critters spin tales of old.

In the candyland hideaway, we roam,
Every sweet tooth dreams of home.
So take a seat on a fondant chair,
And let the sugary stories ensnare.

Sweet Temptations

In a patch of frosted delight,
Ginger critters dance at night.
With frosting hats and sprinkles neat,
They twirl around with tasty feet.

Don't be shy, just take a nibble,
Sugar shivers make you giggle.
Chocolate rivers can be steep,
But laughter echoes, not a peep!

Syrupy rain or gummy flurries,
Every day is filled with stories.
Try not to taste the licorice grass,
For it might turn your giggle to sass.

So flounce with glee and take a chance,
In this world of sweet romance.
Where every turn is made of fun,
And every bite leaves you undone.

Candy Dreams

Close your eyes to the sugary scene,
Where every dream is sweet and keen.
Gummy starships soar so high,
On licorice ropes, we touch the sky.

Marzipan moons glow soft and bright,
Whispering wishes throughout the night.
Chocolate comets zoom with flair,
In this candy mystery, we're unaware.

Waffles dance on syrupy toes,
While jellybeans giggle in rows.
Lollipop lullabies play a tune,
Underneath the cupcake moon.

With candy dreams, we'll never tire,
In lands of joy that inspire.
So let's indulge in this delight,
Where every whim becomes our flight.

The Kingdom of Sweets

In a land where the cupcakes grow tall,
Marshmallows bounce and tumble, oh what a ball!
Lollipops dance with a twist and a twirl,
Gummy bears giggle and give it a whirl.

Chocolate rivers flow like a sweet, sticky dream,
Candy canes bend, it's not what it seems!
Taffy trees swaying in candy-corn breeze,
Welcome to where you're brought to your knees!

Donut-shaped clouds float up in the sky,
Sugar sprinkles rain down, oh my, oh my!
The jelly bean sun gives a bubbly cheer,
In this kingdom, sweet tooth revere!

Here a cake castle makes its bold stand,
Covered in frosting, oh isn't it grand?
But watch for the bites from the cookie king,
He's cheeky and sweet, but likes to take a swing!

Sugary Serenade

Whipped cream mountains rise misty and bright,
Peanut butter paths lead to cuddly delights.
A chorus of caramel sings through the air,
Chocolate chip whispers are sweet as a prayer.

Sprinkled confetti lights up the parade,
You'll trip on a truffle but don't be afraid!
Fudge rivers flow, glistening in the sun,
In this sugary realm, we all have our fun.

Jellybeans bouncing, so lively and spry,
Licorice laughter as they jump and fly.
Soda pop fountains bubble and fizz,
Take a sip and you'll see just what bliss is!

Join the dance of the candied brigade,
In this land where all worries do fade.
Syrupy wishes come true every day,
With confections so sweet, who could ever stray?

Walls of Cookie Canvas

Can you see the walls that are crispy and brown?
Decorated thickly, bright icing renowned.
They're strong as they stand, oh what a display,
But watch out for the snackers who nibble away!

Pillars of pretzels rise up to the sky,
Windows of sugar glass sparkly and spry.
With every sweet biter, the walls wear a grin,
What a funny sight when they tumble right in.

Chocolate chip shingles adorn the sweet roof,
While whipped cream gables provide a fun proof.
An army of gummy guards stands on their post,
To protect the treasure we love the most!

Steps made of shortbread lead up to the door,
To enter this kingdom, just munch some more!
But beware of the cat that's made out of fudge,
He'll sneak up and nibble, and you might just budge!

Frosted Fantasies

In a world where the icing flows out like a stream,
Frosted visions arise, oh what a sweet dream!
Cupcake trees blossom with sprinkles of cheer,
While licorice vines wrap around with a sneer.

Here, gummy worms wiggle, oh what a sight,
While candy corn soldiers stand ready to fight.
A pie-filled parade rolls down candy lane,
With laughter and joy in this sugary domain.

Everyone feasts on a platter of fun,
Pies filled with dreams, oh we're never done!
With donuts for dancing and cakes for the song,
We laugh and we play, come all, join along!

Yet who could resist the sweet cotton candy?
It's fluffy, it's funny, it's just so dandy!
So step to the beat of the sugary trance,
In frosted fantasies, let's laugh and dance!

Enchanted Confections

In a land where sweets grow tall,
Candies dance and lollipops sprawl,
Gumdrop gardens bloom with glee,
A giggly treat for you and me.

Frosted windows, frosting smiles,
Marshmallow clouds, we'll stay a while,
Chocolate streams that flow with cheer,
Let's nibble bits, there's nothing near!

Sugar critters skip and play,
Caramel rivers lead the way,
A cookie cat gives chase with glee,
In this sweet town, we're all so free.

Every bite, a fun surprise,
With sprinkles dancing in our eyes,
So gather round, it's time to munch,
We'll feast on laughter—what a brunch!

The Sugar Shack

In a shack made of candy canes,
Bright licorice drains and candy lanes,
Gummy bears bounce off the walls,
While frosted cupcakes make their calls.

Muffin men with jelly hats,
Dance around with silly spats,
With rainbow sprinkles flying high,
And chocolate bunnies hopping by.

Fudge fountains and licorice whips,
Lemonade from sugar sips,
We giggle while we take a bite,
In our sweet realm, all feels right.

So come and join this laughter feast,
In the shack where joy won't cease,
We'll share our smiles, it's quite a treat,
With candy rhythms, oh so sweet!

Whispers of Frosting

Where frosting swirls in colors bright,
And peppermint dreams take flight at night,
A gingerbread breeze whispers low,
In this land of sweets, let's take it slow.

Cake pop critters whisper secrets,
Waffle trees sway with sweet regrets,
Even the gumdrops have their say,
In this frosting world, we love to play.

Sprinkles chatter, jellybeans laugh,
As we craft our treat-filled path,
With licorice ropes and sugar cheers,
Every giggle echoes through the years.

So close your eyes, let your dreams run wild,
In this candy world where we're all a child,
With laughter swirling in every bite,
We'll dance with sweetness, shining bright.

The Ginger Fortress

Behold the fortress made from sweets,
Where candy guards defend the treats,
A jelly moat surrounds the ground,
In sugary realms, joy's always found.

Gingerbread soldiers stand so proud,
With icing shields, they shout quite loud,
Marshmallow marshals lead the charge,
In this fortress, everything's large!

Candy corn flags wave in the air,
As chocolate knights do battle rare,
Laughing, we cross gumdrop bridges,
Frosty fun that never fridges.

Join the frolic, feast with cheer,
In this kingdom, there's nothing to fear,
With every giggle, the fortress grows,
In our candy fortress, joy just flows!

The Enchanted Bakery Abode

In a land where pies take flight,
Cookies dance under the moonlight.
Marshmallows fluff with a giggle,
And lollipops playing a sneaky wiggle.

Sugar sprinkles fall like rain,
Frolicking donuts in a sugar lane.
The roof is frosted, bright and sweet,
Where candy canes dance on ginger feet.

A muffin cat naps on a floor,
As jellybeans play hide and score.
With icing rivers flowing wide,
Cupcake boats take a joyful ride.

In this place of chewy delight,
Everything's tasty, oh what a sight!
So sip your tea with marshmallow fluff,
In this bakery home, there's never enough!

Lollipop Lattices and Gumdrop Gardens

Under candy clouds, the sun does shine,
Gumdrop gardens, oh so divine.
Lollipop lattices sway in the breeze,
While candy critters dance with ease.

Taffy trees bend with joy,
A chocolate stream, oh what a ploy!
Jellybean flowers bloom in rows,
Each petal a giggle, how it glows!

A licorice bridge, wobbly and round,
Where licorice snakes are often found.
Raise a toast with soda pop,
In this sweet spot, we'll never stop!

Beneath the gumdrops, secrets reside,
Whiskers of sweetness, come take a ride.
Sugary whispers tease at night,
In this garden, everything feels right!

A Sweet Escape in Biscuit Cladding

In a realm where biscuits cling tight,
Crackers soaring to a delight.
Frosting waterfalls cascade down,
While cookie critters wear a crown.

Marzipan walls stand proud and bold,
And candy whispers stories told.
The choco-bricks hold laughs inside,
With jelly bean frogs that hop and glide.

Sprinkle showers dance around,
While biscuit bunnies bounce off the ground.
Candy roofs with a sticky sheen,
In this sweet escape, we reign supreme!

There's always room for one more pie,
With giggles floating in the sky.
Take a nibble off the fun,
In this land where laughter is never done!

Chocolate Riverbeds and Molasses Pathways

Where chocolate rivers twist and swirl,
Gumdrops plop, a sugary whirl.
Molasses pathways lead us astray,
As we dance in decadent play!

Fudge mountains rise with a gooey glow,
While candy corn bunnies hop to and fro.
A licorice airship zooms by,
With a jellybean captain ready to fly!

Scrumptious secrets in every nook,
Chocolate chips waiting in every cook.
Sweets surround us, a jolly parade,
In the sugary bliss, let's not be delayed!

With frothy giggles and joyous cheer,
Each flavor sings, our hearts sincere.
So take the plunge, dip your toes,
In this land where the fun never slows!

The Biscuit Cathedral

In the land where sweets unite,
A cathedral stands, oh what a sight!
With walls of wafer, tall and wide,
And jelly beans as guests inside.

The roof is made of chocolate bars,
Where gummy bears gaze at the stars.
The priest is made of icing, sweet,
With minty shoes upon his feet.

The congregation dances, sways,
To the tune of candy cane displays.
In this realm of sugar rush,
Laughing while the puppies blush.

So come and join the biscuit cheer,
Bring your friends and lots of beer!
In a place where laughter grows,
And as sweet as it ever goes.

Sweet Tooth Sanctuary

Welcome to the sanctuary, stand in line,
Where every flavor's simply divine.
A marshmallow plush, a lollipop tree,
Where unicorns giggle and say, "Have some tea!"

The floors are made from cookie dough,
With frosting rivers that ebb and flow.
A wise old cupcake presides with grace,
While crayons and jelly bop in place.

The air is thick with strawberry cream,
As licorice whispers flirt and beam.
Fizzy drinks in glasses of glass,
Watch out for the gumball that could pass!

In this haven, laughter spins,
Candy-scented futures begin!
Slip on gumdrops, let out a cheer,
In a sanctuary without any fear.

The Candy Coated Haven

In a haven coated sweet and bright,
Candies dance under the moonlight.
Marshmallow clouds float up so high,
As licorice whips loop and fly.

To the left, a chocolate swing,
Where gobstoppers whirl and sing.
The dragon's breath is cotton candy,
Mischief lurks—oh, isn't it dandy?

Here, every door is made of gum,
A silly place where we all come.
Pop rocks crackle with every step,
While jelly tots giggle, in prep!

Join the frolic, join the fun,
In a haven where surprises run.
With laughter ringing, spirits soar,
Let's live it up and beg for more!

Pastry Paradise

In pastry paradise, we all belong,
Where cookies hum their favorite song.
With donut holes that spin and glide,
And sweet relish pickles on the side.

The fountains flow with soda pop,
While licorice vines twist and hop.
The sun is a cupcake, frosted bright,
In this comical, sugary light.

Watch out for the raspberry squad,
As they giggle and share a nod.
Muffins bloom in the wild, oh dear!
While sour patch friends spread good cheer.

Pastry chefs dance in their aprons tight,
Whipping up treats from morning till night.
Dive into joy, where flavors collide,
In pastry paradise, let's take a ride!

Hearth of Honeyed Dreams

In a cottage of sugar, where laughter resides,
Candy corns giggle and laughter collides.
With gumdrop doors that squeak and swing,
Every corner hides a delightful thing.

Marshmallow pillows and jellybean treats,
Gingerbread men dance on sugary streets.
With frosting rivers that flow with glee,
All dreams are sweet as they dance by the tree.

Chocolate chip windows, bright as the sun,
Every nibble taken is just the best fun.
Licorice ropes tied in knots for a game,
In this joyful abode, never the same.

So come take a peek, but don't take a bite,
For the candy's alive with a whimsical light.
In the warmth of the hearth, both cozy and bright,
Honeyed dreams linger, a charming delight.

Candy-Coated Memories

In a land where the lollipops grow on tall trees,
And sodas run wild in the sweet summer breeze.
Where memories stick like caramel glue,
Every flavor a story, a tale tried and true.

Bubblegum laughter fills the air every day,
As cupcakes with sprinkles swim and sway.
Gumdrop paths lead us right to the fun,
With a sprinkle of joy, we race 'til we're done.

Jellybean jests that make everyone smile,
Marzipan friends who stay for a while.
In this candy-coated world, don't be shy,
Where the only limit is how high you can fly.

Take a stroll down the chocolate chip lane,
Where giggles and sweetness will make you insane.
Each moment a snapshot, a smile and a cheer,
In candy-coated memories, we hold them so dear.

Specters of Sweetness in Every Nook

Ghosts of gumdrops float in the air,
A ghastly delight with frosting to spare.
They laugh and they dance on this sugary ground,
With every sweet haunt, giggles abound.

Chocolate bats flutter, their wings all aglow,
In this spooky abode, we'll put on a show.
Lollipop lanterns light up the night,
With specters of sweetness, a whimsical fright.

Hiding in corners, the candy corn creeps,
Whispering secrets as everyone sleeps.
Fudge phantoms prance, swirling around,
In the heart of this treat, joy can be found.

So fear not the sweets that come in the night,
For they're just here to make spirits bright.
In every sweet shadow, a giggle will bloom,
With specters of sweetness, we chase away gloom.

Frosted Façades and Dreams of Dessert

Built from icing and dreams, a sweet little sight,
With frosted façades that gleam in the light.
Where candy canes line every whimsical way,
And desserts are the stars, in a scrumptious ballet.

Marshmallow clouds drift in a sugary sky,
While cookie cutters dance and don't even try.
The frosting flows freely, a river of cheer,
In this whimsical world, there's nothing to fear.

Gumdrops and licorice twirl 'round and round,
In this land of delights where happiness is found.
Every slice of pie sings a jubilant tune,
Like a birthday party every day in June.

So come, take a seat at the candy buffet,
Where laughter is served on a platter divine.
In frosted façades, where fondness abounds,
The dreams of dessert are the sweetest of sounds.

The Ginger Cottage Chronicles

In a field of sugar dreams, it stands tall,
With candy cane pillars, it beckons all.
The roof is a rainbow, the walls, pure delight,
Come taste the adventure, and stay for the bite.

But beware of the crumbs that lead to a trap,
Where licorice rats might give you a clap.
A gumdrop butler serves tea with a grin,
While marshmallow fluff spills, where chaos begins.

Lollipop lamps light up every nook,
As gumdrop gardens hide secrets in book.
You'd think it was perfect, no worries or fuss,
Until frosting grows legs and begins to discuss!

Oh, the stories this cottage could gleefully tell,
Of chocolate chip rain and a jellybean spell.
So come set your compass to sweet and absurd,
In this wacky abode where laughter's assured.

Frosting Fantasies and Spice-Scented Secrets

A realm where the frosting flows thick like a stream,
And cinnamon clouds bring each moment a dream.
Peppermint whispers tickle your ears,
As cupcakes confide all their sweet little fears.

The curtains are made of spun sugar delight,
They flutter with giggles in the soft morning light.
Nutmeg-nosed gnomes dance on candy cane floors,
While jellybean critters peek through the doors.

But oh, what a mess when the rain starts to fall,
The licorice pipes burst, and it's sticky for all!
In this charming domain where whimsy is king,
Baking becomes an outrageous fling!

So put on your apron, and let's start the fun,
In our sugary kingdom, there's joy for everyone!
With toppings galore and humor in piles,
We'll laugh all the way through these frosting-filled miles.

Crumbly Corners of Comfort

In the crannies and nooks of this sugary place,
Sit gingerbread folks with a smile on each face.
The walls made of cookie are cozy and warm,
And laughter is bustling like bees in a swarm.

With frosting for pillows and sprinkles for sheets,
The inhabitants gather for fantastical feats.
They play hide and seek, dodging crumbs on the floor,
But beware of the bites from the gummy bear's roar!

When twilight descends, and the moon's made of pie,
The residents frolic, their spirits so high.
Chocolate fountains bubble and sing a sweet tune,
While gumdrops perform a most colorful swoon.

So step into this realm where the funny collides,
With sugary magic, true joy never hides.
This world made of wonder, of sweetness and cheer,
Will tickle your senses and bring laughter near.

A Scent of Vanilla Clouds

Oh, the air is alive with vanilla-sweet charms,
As laughter ignites like the coziest arms.
A landscape of icing, all fluffy and light,
Cradles our spirits in soft, sweet delight.

The sun's a warm cookie, the sky drizzled glaze,
Each breeze filled with giggles that tickle and blaze.
With fudge-flavored rainbows and sherbet-green grass,
Life in this haven is nothing but sass!

A troupe of gumdrops keep juggling snacks,
While icing-topped critters plan sly little hijacks.
In marshmallow meadows, they dance and they play,
With cookies for kites that float joyfully away.

So come take a stroll, let your worries all melt,
In this whimsical world, where true joy is felt.
With each giggling step through this savory shroud,
You'll soar on the warmth of vanilla-clouded loud!

Milton Keynes UK
Ingram Content Group UK Ltd.
UKHW020043271124
451585UK00012B/1030